This Easy Falling

poems by

Tom Raithel

Finishing Line Press
Georgetown, Kentucky

This Easy Falling

Copyright © 2023 by Tom Raithel
ISBN 979-8-88838-228-8 First Edition
All rights reserved under International and Pan-American Copyright Conventions. No part of this book may be reproduced in any manner whatsoever without written permission from the publisher, except in the case of brief quotations embodied in critical articles and reviews.

ACKNOWLEDGMENTS

Thanks to the editors of the following journals in which the following poems first appeared, sometimes in slightly different versions or with different titles:

Atlanta Review: "March," "On a Winter Night."
Coneflower Café: "Patterns."
The Evening Street Review: "In Praise of Mud."
Midwest Quarterly: "The Beast," "High Summer," "Holiday," "A New Language," "Starlings," "This Easy Falling," and "What the River Told Me."
Open 24 Hours: "Mirror," "Stars."
The Southern Review: "Cumulus."
Tipton Poetry Journal: "Children of the Wind," "The Deer," "Equinox," "The Readers,"

Thanks to Matthew Graham, Jim McGarrah and Tom Wilhelmus, for organizing the RopeWalk Writers Retreat, from which I learned so much.

Thanks to the many consultants and workshop leaders who taught me, including Ada Limon, Robert Wrigley, Kim Addonizio, Stephen Dobyns, Heather McHugh, Andrew Hudgins and David Wojahn.

Thanks, too, to Maggie Smith for help in manuscript editing and preparation.

And special thanks to members of First Mondays—Linda Neal Reising, Mark Williams, Jessica Thompson, Teresa Roy and Barbara Bennett—my companions in poetry.

Publisher: Leah Huete de Maines
Editor: Christen Kincaid
Cover Art: Jessica D. Thompson
Author Photo: Joel Hauserman
Cover Design: Elizabeth Maines McCleavy

Order online: www.finishinglinepress.com
also available on amazon.com

Author inquiries and mail orders:
Finishing Line Press
PO Box 1626
Georgetown, Kentucky 40324
USA

Table of Contents

When We Were Stars 1

On a Winter Night 2

New Year's Day 3

Starlings 4

Mirror 5

Patterns 6

The Lake 7

March 8

Children of the Wind 9

The Readers 10

Rain 11

In Praise of Mud 12

What the River Told Me 13

Cumulus 14

Shape-shifter 15

The Deer 16

Hawk 17

The Beast 18

High Summer 19

The Flies 20

Eyes 21

Stars 22

Holiday 23

Equinox 24

This Easy Falling 25

A New Language 26

for George and Marion Raithel

When We Were Stars

> *The atoms of our bodies are traceable to stars that exploded...*
> *across our galaxy billions of years ago.*
> —Neil deGrasse Tyson

When we were stars, we burned with a fury
that blew back the darkness and shattered the void.

We wheeled and blazed with a violent will
through nights of cosmic confusion,

spinning along with galactic lovers,
friends and strangers—companions in chaos.

Out of our fire, we begot planets,
comets and moons. We whirled in joy.

We'd heard of death—the dread supernova—
but it seemed distant. Then, it was near.

We burned on, though, secure in the faith
that we'd rise again and know the old fury—

perhaps with a hand, a voice, or a face.
We'd be something star-like, but brilliantly new.

On a Winter Night

Stand long enough in the winter night
and you enter a vast but intimate landscape.

Stars like ice. Wind-lashed pines.
The snow-framed faces of distant houses.

Watching your breath disperse in darkness,
you feel winter creep through your coated warmth.

Listen for the hushed footfall of the fawn.
Follow the flight of the moon-eyed owl.

Welcome night into your lungs, your blood.
Let the gusts bury your thoughts in snow

until you discover the deeper aloneness,
the emptier cold, the heavier darkness.

Then you will come to know your kinship
with owl, with fawn, with ice-bound house,

with stubborn pine and resolute star,
as you stand in the winter night.

New Year's Day

A blast of alarm and a flurry of blankets.
Bare feet plod over chilled, wood floor.

Fingernail branches scratch at the window.
Snow squalls spatter and hiss.

And neither warm toast nor the steam of coffee
can quell the vortex within.

Resolved: To keep moving. To shower. To shave.
To dress in a way that disguises failure.

Then out the door onto sleet-slick street,
ice-braided whirlwinds lashing your coat.

Further resolved: To walk slow or slide.
To rise with invectives whenever you slip.

To remember to count every fall a success
as long as you're willing to fall down again.

The cough of ignition. The grumble of gears.
Tires crunching soot-crusted snow.

Then to the highway, ramping up speed,
the refuse of last year tumbling behind you.

Starlings

So you drive a long day on the mid-winter highway,
gray fields around you, gray skies ahead,
your hands sluggish and slack on the wheel,
the highway unchanging, no motion, no sound,
except for the drone of your wheels on the road,
the wind as you drive. Suddenly—

starlings—a burst of black lightning,
a fluttering storm, a thousand-winged wave,
raising an air-borne archway above you
that swivels, surges, veers and is gone—

and your day is remade, though you drive the same highway,
gray fields and skies now vibrant ahead.

Mirror

Here is your forest pool hung on the wall,
a portrait of you with adjustable pose,
the window on one room you can never enter
though one you are already in.

You consult it daily, religiously even,
standing within its gaze like a shadow,
the bedroom behind you now cast in front,
the light of the world bent backward.

It tells you your shirt and pants match today.
Your collar is crooked. Attractively roguish?
Your hair's a mess. Pat it down there.
Is that just the light? New gray?

But no matter how deeply you peer,
of itself it tells you nothing.
A perfect companion—honest but silent.
All reflections will be about you,

beholding you not as you are, exactly,
but as an immortal might see you—
you as a phantom, a short-lived brightness,
a flicker, a flourish, a trick of the light.

Patterns

Woven by hands of Moroccan women
with an eye for fabric and feel for design

and patterned with colors and abstract forms,
this rich, rectangular rug.

Patterns of squares with patterns inside—
symmetrical beasts, crystalline flowers

and trees with triangular, bright-winged birds.
Across this rug, the patterns repeat

just as the musical patterns repeat
in the Mozart piano concerto that plays

as my hand and pen scratch on my notebook
patterns that stand for meaningful sound.

So we make patterns to catch and please
our eyes, ears and well-nerved bodies,

patterns lifted from the curved weave
of the mulberry branch, from the wind's song,

from footprints written in snow that lead
to the backward glance of the fox.

The Lake
    (after Lu Chi's The Way to Write)

Within me, there is a quiet lake
that I go to whenever I can.

Surrounded by pines and murmuring reeds,
it teems with the life of poems.

When I launch my canoe on its smooth surface,
I float atop memorable peaks of the past.

Above me, musical truths take flight,
whose course I follow, paddle in hand.

I fish for the most fit words and images.
I drink clear water from a shining cup.

When the sun drops over western forests,
I row to the shore, pull up my canoe

and build a small fire of inspired flame,
cooking my poem till firm and sweet.

I listen to loons call out from the water
till the lake within me falls silent and sleeps.

March

Out of a gray depression of sky,
a cold rain falls. Stark, black branches

shake in rough wind. The birdbath is toppled.
The wood fence gapped. The garden,

the stonework in ruins. Meanwhile old friends,
like last year's leaves, lie scattered all over,

or under the earth. Above these floodwaters,
hunched on a limb, a crow now broods.

It's been here before. It knows what to do.
All we know is to fasten our jackets,

bend like a branch to the buffeting wind,
grope like a root in the cold, wet ground.

Children of the Wind

They love to hide, but you hear their whispers
as they run through grass or climb into trees.

They'll topple a yard sign, knock off a hat,
or scatter a neighbor's leaves through your yard.

Bored and ignored by grown-ups before,
and lured by a sense of adventure,

they stepped out one day into open air,
and the air took them in. Spirits now,

they're not afraid of the dark anymore.
They won't come in when called.

On bad days, though, you hear them cry,
mourning their loss of embraceable form.

Then they may rush up to you on your walk
and hug you with gusty arms.

The Readers

At tables and desks, surrounded by bookshelves,
they bend to their screens and pages,
silently drinking words with their eyes.

Rainbowed coronas swell around their heads,
and inside each—a separate world.
Here, a physicist chalks an equation.

There, a birdwatcher catalogs sparrows.
Now the conductor finds blood on luggage
as the train steams through Siberian night.

Though thunder outside resounds through the library,
readers stay fixed to their spheres
until one closes her book with a thud,

bursting her cloud. Its residue falls.
When she walks out to the rain-soaked street,
dust of the rainbow clings to her eyes.

Rain

Out of the body sprawled on the sidewalk,
blood runs away in absolving rain.

A rain of desire taps out a tune
on the roof of the honeymoon cottage.

Within the cove of a cardboard shanty,
a vagrant waits out the rain of the poor

while at the manor, silver rain
mars the blue sheen of the private pool.

Boys run away in a laughing rain.
Solemn rain darkens the hospice windows.

A thief's rain lashes the purse-snatcher's coat.
Cold rain of law pounds the judge's casement.

On broken buildings and bodies contorted—
the smoldering rain of war.

After the funeral, lyrical rain—
a robin calls through the dripping leaves.

In Praise of Mud

Child of snowmelt and copious rain,
nursed on manure and leaf-rot,

you bless our lawns, sidewalks and roads
with your ample and opulent brown.

We walk in your richness, which clings to our shoes.
We carry you into our shops and homes.

We plunge our hands into your lush ooze
and sow you with seed. We care for you.

Though plain and smelling of worms and must,
you glorify us with lilacs and roses.

The wealth of grass depends on you,
the intricate wisdom of roots and branches.

Within your grit, both life and death—
the graveyard becomes you as well as the garden.

Generously, you lend us our flesh,
which, one day, we'll return to you.

What the River Told Me

        You try too hard, my struggling friend.
      You're far too rigid, grasping and proud.
Let yourself go on a humbler course,

following the ancient pull of the world.
    Flow down summits and weed-thick slopes,
        across pebbled bottoms and streaming sands.

Lend yourself freely to reeds and lilies
    where dragonflies hunt and green frogs hide.
        Roll easily into mudflats and marshes,

        lakes and lagoons where pickerel sleep,
    where buck and blue heron bend down to drink.
This low-lying modesty becomes you.

        Nourish the shaded groves and grasslands
    that cattle graze, the columns of corn.
Surrender yourself to gardens and lawns—

your gifts will be returned in kind.
    Fulfill the harbors, shipyards and mills.
        Give to what seeks you, whatever thirsts.

Cumulus

> *Hamlet: Do you see yonder cloud that's almost in shape of a camel?*
> *Polonius: By th'mass, and 'tis like a camel indeed.*
> *Hamlet: Methinks it is like a weasel.*
> *Polonius. It is backed like a weasel.*
> *Hamlet: Or like a whale.*
> *Polonius: Very like a whale.*
> —*Shakespeare*

Forget the old science of water droplets
clinging to sky-blown dust.

The truth is these are the sailboats of gods,
climbing and crossing waves of sky

in a race to the borders of daylight.
See how their sails turn red at sunset?

Then again, these seem less like sails
than wind, than the misty breath of giants

snoring under the rocks and forests,
shaking the world in their sleep.

Actually, though, they're less like breath
than words, than airmailed messages

sent by lakes to faraway mountains.
I wish I could crack their code.

The truth really is they're flying islands,
mirrors of thought, lakes in the sky,

modeling clay for cherubs and angels,
airliners filled with traveling dreams.

Shape-shifter

The shape-shifter never loses an hour
shopping for shirts and slacks that fit.

No diets. No workouts to flatten the abs.
No aisle too narrow. No shelf too high.

Missing a bus, it sprouts hawk wings
and glides above highways of honking traffic.

Shut from a room where rivals conspire,
it hangs, spider-like, in vents and listens.

Drawbacks are few. An identity crisis.
Always the visitor, never at home.

But all the world's corners lie open, ready,
as it moves, a chameleon, among us.

Or travels beyond us, bounding up mountains
in four-footed glee to bay at the moon,

or swimming the shadowed, shipwrecked depths
to lift lost treasures in tentacled arms.

The Deer

They look so lost, staring in windows,
or standing wide-eyed by a neighbor's pool,
or stumbling up to a boulevard island,
pausing and gawking at cars around them.

With heads high or close to the ground,
they wander as if looking for something,
a highway sign for a homebound exit,
a key they dropped to a door now closed.

A car honk startles. Sharp ears erect,
they take trembling steps, unsure what to do,
then quicken their long-legged trek through a world
that won't welcome, nor leave them alone.

They lie down at night on some golf-course green
or brambly edge of a railroad yard
and dream of a brook through a columbine meadow,
moonlight breezing through pine.

Hawk

> *For beauty is nothing*
> *but the beginning of terror*
> *—Rainer Maria Rilke*

Born of the marriage of lightning terror
to the beauty of wide, blue sky,
the hawk glides down over roofs and yards,
a barbarous brilliance, an elegant outlaw,
a murderous heart in an angel's frame.
Wings extended, dark eyes bright,
talons flaring, open, outstretched,
it cuts off the flight of a mourning dove
in a flutter of feathers and blood—
a violence that so offends the day
the air will only recover its stillness
when the hawk, death still warm in its grasp,
wings its way gracefully up to high branches,
bends down its beak and feeds.

The Beast

As sullen as darkness, as surly as wind,
it's out there tonight, awake and hungry.

Maybe far off under desert stars,
some place where coyotes snarl over bones,

it stretches its limbs, yawns its cat mouth,
leaps from a rock and begins a long trek.

Maybe even as you read by lamplight,
its green eyes and perked ears search.

You'll never see it until it sees you,
and when it sees you, you've seen it too late.

Across dusty gulches and stony arroyos,
it stalks with a muscular, padded tread.

Into the foothills and up rocky peaks,
the sure-footed bighorn scampering aside.

Over iced slopes and trout-rippled streams,
into pine forests and stubble fields

where yelping dogs bring out a half-dressed farmer,
who levels his shotgun—nothing is there.

Into the suburbs and cities it strides,
into the scrap-yards and rubbish-strewn streets.

A stirring of shadows? A tap at your window?
Probably only a moth at the screen.

Relax. A moth. There's nothing to see.
Besides, when you see it, you've seen it too late.

High Summer

Our eyes were born for such generous sunlight,
our bodies to breathe such congenial air.

A high blue sky. A couple of clouds.
Songbirds in trees of vigorous green.

On a morning like this, the man shoveling dirt
feels as though he could lift a mountain,

while the woman who waters tomato seedlings
believes they will grow forever.

Who sees the girl on the back porch sobbing?
The day-moon sharp as an uplifted knife?

The Flies

Tiny, black heralds on netherworld wings
descend on our summer,

droning their monotone song.
They desire only our undesired—

rotting road-kill, fallen fruit,
festering back-alley dumpster.

Millions of eyes without expression,
they labor with neither disgust nor affection,

their manner as fleeting, indifferent and dark
as the prophecy they deliver

to the kitchen window, the bedroom curtain,
the soft, sweet skin of a baby's arm.

Eyes

Eyes of the angry hurl scarlet flames.
Black smoke curls in their brows.

Eyes of the hurt shut themselves in dark rooms
with weeping and banging of fists.

Sunrise glows in the eyes of the hopeful.
Songbirds flit through the April branches.

Perfumed smiles and glimmering words
mask the seducer's lustful eyes.

Eyes of the jealous have hooks and snares.
Prisoners pace in their dungeons.

The moonless night of the graveyard looms
in the flinching eyes of the fearful.

Eyes of the proud flaunt polished trophies.
Eyes of the wise pass by and smile.

Glittering gold in eyes of the greedy
is vaulted within a grimacing skull.

Stars

Look for them, and they vanish.
But they'll come to you indirectly,

out of the twilight corners.
Simply sit back on your evening porch,

and let your eyes wander the blue horizon
into the August night.

Hear the deep-weeded dirge of crickets?
Laughter fading from nearby yards?

Soon you dissolve and the wind recedes.
House lights go out. The night grows cold.

And there, above the far glow of the city,
another star falls. Then another.

The others, too—the ones that don't fall—
are turning their secret pages.

Holiday

This is how we should always live—
our days unclouded and easy.

Now, while a veil of late summer haze
softens a trestled and towered skyline,

we watch white sails cross a blue horizon
as waves lather glistening sand.

Swim-suited lovers splash one another
and fall into shoreline foam.

Slicked-up sunbathers bake their backs
or read on beach chairs, drinks in hand.

Even the gulls seem to take the day off,
watching the world from mooring posts.

When the sun melts into smoldering oils
and the shoreline grows dark, deserted and cold,

we'll sit around fires and re-tell our stories
to the stars and the rhythmic hush of waves.

Equinox

Maybe the way the half-moon lingers,
pale as a ghost in the bloodstained dawn,

or the way that cloud, once iridescent,
seems like sackcloth weighted with ash.

The trees look older and sadder today.
Larcenist winds are stealing the gold.

Birds, contemplating all things from a wire,
are shrouded in cloaks of apocalypse.

All the roads wander, void of desire.
Houses have sunk into fitful sleep.

Over the broken latch of a gate,
a spider spins a foreboding sign.

You understand things will be different tomorrow,
the air more bitter, the light more lean,

and when you walk out under cold, new skies,
you must be different, too.

This Easy Falling

This is their ruin,
   their beauty, too,
      this easy falling,

making a silent
   but resonant music.
      One at a time—

russet, bronze,
   golden or bruised—
      prompting us sometimes

to take in a breath
   or linger a while
      at a window.

Each leaf a separate,
   thin-veined brightness—
      a friendship, a love,

something we once
   were able to do
      but no longer can.

Each leaf a piece
   of the tree's rich being,
      now in the air,

now in the mud,
   now on the sidewalk
      under our feet.

A New Language

Before I die,
I want to learn

October's language,
its colorful accents

and somber tones.
I want to speak

with the soft baritone
of the wind sweeping

through ocher woods,
the clear consonant

of the acorn's drop.
I'll study the conjugations

of geese, crossing the sky
in wedge-shaped flocks

and learn the crimson
declensions of sunset.

I'll understand how
a question is posed

by the absence of swallows,
an exclamation

by the first fall of snow.
Before I die

I'll learn to read,
along dusky branches,

the hieroglyphics
of crows.

Tom Raithel grew up in Milwaukee, Wisconsin and earned bachelor's and master's degrees at the University of Wisconsin-Milwaukee. He has worked as a busboy, assembly-line worker, truck-loader, janitor, landscaper and public relations specialist, as well as a journalist for several newspapers in the Midwest. His poems have appeared in *The Southern Review, Midwest Quarterly, Atlanta Review, Nimrod, The Comstock Review, Southern Poetry Review* and other journals. His work was selected for the Ohio River Valley Edition of The Boom Project: *Voices of a Generation*. Finishing Line Press published his first chapbook, *Dark Leaves, Strange Light*. Today he lives in Cleveland, Ohio, with his wife, Theresa Brett.

www.ingramcontent.com/pod-product-compliance
Lightning Source LLC
Chambersburg PA
CBHW022127090426
42743CB00008B/1045